Everything You Need to Know About

DEALING WITH LOSSES

Loss and change can be scary. But there are many steps you can take to get through it.

· THE NEED TO KNOW LIBRARY ·

Everything You Need to Know About

DEALING WITH LOSSES

Stefanie Iris Weiss

THE ROSEN PUBLISHING GROUP, INC.
NEW YORK

To the three most divinely inspirational women I know: Ora Ben-Aviv, Elizabeth
  Goldman, and Sherene Shostack. With them in my life, I never stop learning.

I owe immeasurable thanks to those in my life who have stood by me with compassion
and boundless love through my own many and loudly-vocalized losses: Mom, Hal,
Nanny, Jodi, Liz G., Liz S., Missy, Nancy, Ora, Rachelle, Sherene, and my precious poetry students. Props to the Grey Dog for endless cups of coffee.

Published in 1998 by The Rosen Publishing Group, Inc.
29 East 21st Street, New York, NY 10010

First Edition
Copyright © 1998 by The Rosen Publishing Group, Inc.

Library of Congress Cataloging-in-Publication Data

Weiss, Stefanie Iris.
    Everything you need to know about dealing with losses / Stefanie iris Weiss.
    p.   cm. — (The need to know library)
    Includes bibliographical references and index.
    Summary: Describes different kinds of losses, including the death of a loved
  one, the end of a love affair, and the loss of virginity, and suggests such coping
  mechanisms as the natural grieving process, the finding of a creative outlet, and
  getting help from others.
    ISBN 0-8239-2780-6
    1. Loss (Psychology) in adolescence—Juvenile literature. 2. Grief in adolescence—
Juvenile literature. [1. Loss (Psychology) 2. Grief.] I. Title. II. Series.
    BF724.3.L66W45 1998
    155.9'37—dc21   98-8496
                                                                           CIP
                                                                            AC

Manufactured in the United States of America.

Contents

Introduction

People usually associate the term loss with the type of grief you go through when someone you love dies. Although the death of a loved one is a devastating kind of loss, people still experience a loss every time their life changes.

Whether you move to a new town, break up with a girlfriend or boyfriend, or even when you lose your virginity, you suffer a loss. Your life changes when you or someone you love gets sick, when your parents get divorced, or when a pet dies.

You've probably already experienced loss in some way. Maybe you didn't think it was okay to grieve, or even think it was that important. But it is.

Everyone experiences loss differently. There is no map for going through the process. Reading this book, you will learn that you are not alone. You will also learn about all the resources available to teenagers who need help dealing with loss. Many of these resources you can build yourself, such as increasing your self-esteem and creating your own support system. Others you can find from counseling or organized support groups.

From this book you will learn, most of all, how to cope and become a stronger, healthier you.

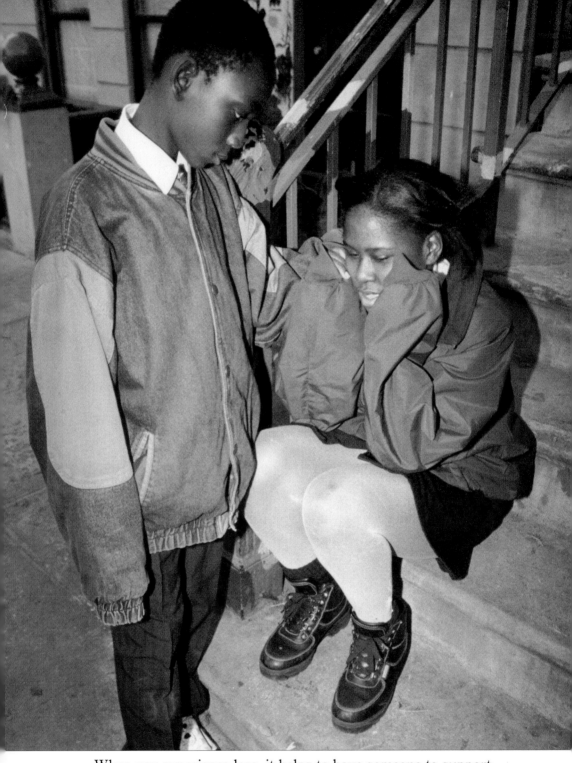

When you experience loss, it helps to have someone to support you.

Chapter 1

What Is Loss?

Loss is change. Change can be healthy and necessary. But sometimes it hurts, and you resist it.

The end of childhood is usually the first form of loss you go through. When you are young enough to believe in Santa Claus and the tooth fairy, you are probably still too young to understand all the implications of loss. But at some point you realize that these things were imaginary instead of real. This may be when you lose your innocence for the first time.

Rites of Passage

Rites of passage help you understand the world as you grow and change. A rite of passage is an experience or ritual that people go through as they travel from childhood to adulthood.

Usually a person's culture determines how he or she marks rites of passage. Some rites of passage are societal,

As a teen, you can look back and see how your ideas about what's real have changed.

such as five-year-olds starting kindergarten. Some are religious rites of passage, like Jewish children have a bar or bat mitzvah when they turn thirteen.

There are differences in rites of passage according to different cultures. For example, in many societies there is an elaborate ceremony when a young woman gets her period. Changes related to sexuality are causes for celebration. This provides young people with a healthy way to deal with conflicting and confusing emotions.

In American culture there are fewer institutionalized rites of passage than in other parts of the world. For example, in America, young girls experience a whirlwind of confusing emotions when they menstruate for the first time, but there is no official observance to mark the event. They have to devise their own coping mechanisms—telling their moms, older sisters, or some other trusted female, and hope that they will gain support and learn the correct information. Sometimes this makes loss and change difficult to work through.

Kellie is the most popular girl in the tenth grade at Kennedy High School. Besides being popular, she is also kind and smart. She started dating Todd, the cutest guy on the lacrosse team and a senior, three months ago. She really likes him. In fact, she thinks she might be in love with him but she's not sure what that means yet. All her friends started having sex when they were in eighth grade, and Kellie always felt like an outsider.

On Friday night, Kellie and Todd were at her house. Her parents went away for the weekend, and Kellie asked Todd to stay over. She was planning to have sex with him. He never pressured her, but she knew he wanted to. Her friends had told her what sex was like, and she had seen lots of soap operas, so she thought she knew what to expect. But losing her virginity wasn't at all what she had hoped.

The next morning, Kellie was depressed. She wanted Todd to leave before they even had breakfast. She felt really sad and she didn't understand why. After Todd left, she went upstairs to her room and pulled the pink teddy bear she had hidden the night before out of her closet. She climbed onto her bed and hugged it and cried. Later that day, she wrote for a long time in her

No matter what kind of loss you have gone through, you need time to work through it.

journal. She felt a little better. Then she called her best friend.

Kellie's emotions are like those of most young men and women after they have lost their virginity. It's not all high fives, like in the movies and on television. Sex is a deeply intimate experience that changes who you are.

Maybe Kellie wasn't ready to have sex. But even if she were ready, her life has been changed forever. She needs to think about the self she has left behind.

Many kinds of loss have flip sides that can be viewed positively. For example, if your sexuality is built on love and trust with another person, you will continue to have healthy relationships when you're older. Maybe some-day you'll even start a family.

Levels of Loss

There are many kinds of loss. Some kinds of loss, like a sibling moving out of the house or a parent leaving because of divorce, might seem easier than others, like a parent dying or a friend committing suicide.

While there different levels of loss, all kinds of loss-es are important. Losing a pet to illness, or a best friend to her new boyfriend, hurts too.

When you experience small losses, your friends and family might tell you to be strong, that it isn't so bad. Or they might not acknowledge your loss at all. But no mat-ter what kind of loss you go through, you still have to work through it. That's why it's so important to recognize loss when it happens in your life. You can talk about it, think about it, and write about it until you feel good again.

There will be more discussion later of some of the coping mechanisms that you can use for loss, like therapy and journal writing. For now, let's look at different kinds of loss in more detail.

Chapter 2

Kinds of Loss

Everyone seems to experience little losses every day. You get back a test that you thought you had aced, and the grade is lower than you expected. Or a teacher calls on you and you don't know the answer—or you answer the question, and the teacher tells you how wrong you are. Your mom yells at you for not taking out the garbage. Whenever you go through something that hurts even a little bit, it makes a difference in your life. But these kinds of losses are relatively easy to recover from. After a few minutes, or in some cases a few hours, these incidents are usually forgotten.

But sometimes things happen that are beyond our control, and they can feel totally devastating.

Illness and Death

The situation that most people associate with the word loss is the loss connected to death and dying. The death of a parent or grandparent is an especially painful experience for teenagers. In the middle of all the trials and tribulations of growing up, suddenly they have to face life without the person who gave them life and raised them.

As a result, when a teen loses a parent or grandparent, he or she often re-experiences what it is like to be a child—totally helpless and dependent. And at the same time, teens may feel as if they have to grow up right away—grow all the way up. This is true even if there is another parent still alive and able to care for them, or if they have other adult role models, or even if they didn't feel close to their parent who died.

Illness is another form of loss. Many teens are forced to deal with illness that has stricken a loved one. Taking care of a parent, grandparent, or sibling in the home can be very stressful.

Coping with illness affects your emotions. You may feel as if you have to be cheerful all the time, because you want to be positive around the sick person. But inside, you may feel like crying because it's hard work and it hurts to see someone so helpless. When a sick person is in the hospital you may feel frustrated because his or her well-being seems beyond your control.

You also may think about what it would be like if that person died, and all the things you ever did or said that weren't so great. It's normal to have feelings of guilt and fear. They are part of the change that's going on around and inside you.

When someone you love dies, you need time to grieve and work through your loss.

Sometimes you're the one who is ill. Teenagers come down with diseases too, although they tend to think of themselves as invincible. They are stricken by cancer, HIV, and other long-term illnesses.

There are ways to treat these diseases. But when you learn of illness, and the whole time you're fighting to get well, it is a time of tremendous strain and change.

Losing Love

Since we've been talking about what it feels like to lose someone you love to death or illness, we should also touch on the other kinds of loss of love.

Many kids come from what are called "broken homes." This most often means a single-parent home.

This can happen because of divorce or death. Some parents just leave with no explanation. Some kids get to know and love a parent who moves away, and some kids never get to know their parents at all.

Many homes are broken by verbal, physical, or sexual abuse. Kids who come from abusive homes live under the constant threat of pain and loss. Usually they live in fear.

Abuse is deeply destructive, and it's more common than anyone imagined. When a parent or another trusted adult berates, beats up on, or sexually molests a child, the full meaning of the damage they inflicted may not come out until years later.

For years Donna's mom wouldn't let her hang out with guys. She always said, "No dating until you're sixteen, Donna!" Now that Donna's sixteenth birthday had passed, she told Robert that she could finally go out with him.

The first few times Donna and Robert hung out, they didn't touch at all. Robert could tell how nervous Donna was. Donna really didn't know why she was so nervous. Her friends had explained how natural and easy it was to kiss a boy.

On Saturday night they went to see a band, and afterward Robert kissed her in the front seat of his car. Suddenly Donna had a flashback to when she was a little girl. She remembered when her Uncle Joe was babysitting for her in their old house. She had a single flash of memory that made her feel sick. It all came flooding back. Her uncle, who now lives in another state, had sexually molested her when she was five years old. That's why she felt so afraid of being even remotely sexual with Robert. She started to cry. Robert didn't understand what was going on. Donna said, "I have to go home right now."

The next morning Donna confronted her mother with her memory. Her mom looked shocked; she turned completely white. Donna was afraid that she wouldn't believe her. She had spent the whole night crying because she remembered how her uncle had told her not to tell anyone. She couldn't understand how she had done such a good job of blocking it out.

Donna's mom believed her story and set to work on finding out where her uncle lived. They decided to prosecute him, even though it had happened eleven years earlier. They found a therapist who specialized in cases of sexual abuse and recovered memory, and Donna started seeing her twice a week. She slowly was able to confront the problems and fears from the abuse she had experienced in her childhood. It was painful, but Donna knew that she could be strong enough to deal with it and overcome the pain.

Adults who abuse children are mentally ill and need immediate professional help. That's why, even though it's scary to report an adult to another authority figure, it must be done as soon as possible. A child who has

If people use drugs in your home, or if you are abused, you need to tell an adult you trust.

been abused by an adult then becomes partly responsible for making sure that adult can't hurt anyone else.

On Being Different

Not fitting in is another form of loss teens go through. People sometimes make assumptions about who you are based on your ethnicity, gender, and social class. If you look or act different from other people your age, people may be cruel to you. You may feel as if your whole identity—your sense of yourself—is being threatened.

This can happen for many other reasons, too. For example, teens sometimes choose to dress in a certain way because they're into hardcore music or hip-hop. They want to express themselves. Sometimes others are threatened by such creativity, and will lash out at those who are different.

It's scary to go to school every day and be teased, even when you know that people do it out of fear.

Unhealthy Ways to Numb the Pain

Often teenagers turn their pain back inward and start doing things that make them hurt even more.

Emotional pain is a major cause of eating disorders such as anorexia nervosa (self-starvation), bulimia (bingeing on large quantities of food and purging), and compulsive eating (bingeing without purging). When someone has an eating disorder, the obsession with food and body image becomes a substitute for other emotional needs such as support and comfort.

Another way people cope in an unhealthy way is through self-mutilation (cutting the body with a sharp object). This usually happens when a person's emotional pain is so great that inflicting physical pain on himself actually creates diversion and release.

Some teens turn to drugs and alcohol to numb reality. At first drinking or taking drugs may seem like a harmless way to forget about problems for a little while. But often, experimentation leads to the nightmare of drug or alcohol addiction.

These means of coping never heal pain. They only briefly cover it over and in the end make problems that are even more difficult to solve.

If you are suffering from any of these disorders, it is

Some teens turn to alcohol or drugs as an unhealthy way to cope with stress.

very important that you get help as soon as possible. In addition to reading this book, talk to someone you trust. No one has to keep pain inside.

As you can see, loss is a small word that encompasses a wide range of experience and emotion. You can probably add your own story to all the stories of loss you've just read about.

There isn't enough space in any book to describe all the kinds of loss that human beings go through. But it is possible to cover the path to healing. We will do so in the chapters that follow.

Friends can be your biggest allies in dealing with loss.

Chapter 3

Starting to Heal

There are as many different paths to healing from loss as there are shapes of snowflakes! Everyone has a unique experience.

Taking the First Step

The first step is always the hardest. Before you can truly heal your loss and feel whole again, you need to admit that you are hurting and need help.

You may deny that you are hurting, telling people "that's all right, I'm fine" when you really aren't fine at all. Sometimes denying emotions can make it easier to cope with the demands of everyday life. Sometimes you just don't want to sound needy, so you spend most of your time alone. Or you may try to take your mind off the pain by doing some other activity, such as playing basketball or watching television.

You also may be in denial because you are afraid to express emotions. Sometimes people feel silly or embarrassed when they need to cry. Boys and men especially are taught that they're not supposed to show pain or cry.

Denial is very normal, and almost everyone does it at some point. The problem is that denying your emotions doesn't make them go away forever. It just pushes them inside for a little while. With the right support, denial can be overcome.

Think about Donna, whose story we read in chapter two. She was in denial for a long time. In fact, if she totally faced the reality of having been abused by her uncle as a child, it would have made it very hard for her to function in her life as a little girl. She was simply too young. A switch went off in her mind to protect her from her situation.

But finally Donna was able to overcome her denial and fear. She remembered her past when she was mature enough to start dealing with it. And she took the brave step of reaching out for help.

Moving Beyond Denial

Moving beyond denial isn't easy. But getting through it makes you stronger and better able to face the entire grieving process.

Denial exists because people sometimes need it in order to cope with the pain in their lives. Denial can be a tool instead of an obstacle, though. If you can recognize the way denial manifests itself in your life and the

While it's important to hang out with buddies, don't let it replace the important time you need to work out your feelings.

lives of people you care about, you can accept it and deal with it head-on.

Jonathan was the best basketball player at the West Fourth Street courts, even though he was only fourteen. Last summer, he'd play pickup ball at least four days a week. Everyone knew who he was. The other reason he was kind of famous downtown was because of his big brother, Mike. Mike didn't play ball, but he was always hanging out.

On a Friday morning in August, Jonathan woke up because he heard his mother crying in the kitchen. He climbed out of bed and asked her what was wrong. She told him that Mike had been arrested the night before.

The cops had been by earlier to tell her and she could-
n't afford the bail to release him.

Jonathan knew his brother. He was a good kid, even
though he sometimes tried to look tough. He wasn't
capable of hurting anyone, and the cops were saying he
stabbed another boy.

Jonathan didn't know what to say to his mom. He
wanted to hug her but he didn't feel that he could. He
went back to his room and changed to go down to the
courts. He thought about all the people he knew that were
arrested and jailed for crimes they didn't commit. He
started to get angry, but then he just strapped on his
Walkman and got on the train. Jonathan loved his broth-
er, but he didn't think about him for the rest of the day.
He just played ball like it was going out of style.

Everyone Is Different

Denial is not always the first step. Because we all deal
with loss in our own way, we progress through the steps
of the grieving process uniquely. We move through the
levels of grief and loss in the way that makes sense to
us, taking into account who we are and who we have
been.

There is no one "right" way to grieve. But the feelings that people usually go through can be broken down
into roughly five steps:

• Denial
• Anger

- Bargaining
- Depression
- Acceptance

These steps were originally broken down by psychologists to address the process of dealing with death. But they can apply to all kinds of loss.

Five Steps in Action

It may help to understand more about these five steps when you can look at an example. First, let's look at a relatively minor trauma.

For example, imagine what it's like to experience the "trauma of the dead battery." Most people who drive a car know what this feels like. Imagine these five steps of the process from the perspective of a person who discovers that his car won't start in the morning.

1. Denial: When a person first realizes that his car won't start, the first thing he does is try it again! He might check that all the lights were turned off, that the radio and heater hadn't been left on, and then he might turn the key in the ignition and push his foot down on the accelerator at least two or three times. He refuses to believe that his car won't start.

2. Anger: He might yell "Stupid car!" He might slam his fists on the steering wheel. You may have seen your parents react this way when their car has failed to start.

3. Bargaining: This might happen when the person realizes that he's late for work or school. He might say
   "Oh, please, car, if you would just start I promise that
   I'll fill you up with the best gas and get you a fresh
   new battery! Just please get me there on time!"

4. Depression: This is when the person would feel
   despair and hopelessness. He might wonder "What
   am I going to do? Now I'll probably get fired and get
   evicted and my life will be over. There's nothing I can
   do."

5. Acceptance: Now the person is ready to deal with the
   situation. "OK, I'm just going to go inside and call the
   auto club and see if we can get this fixed. I'll take a
   bus to work and let my boss know that I'm going to
   be at least an hour late."

Now imagine these steps when there is a deeper trauma
in your life, such as a romantic breakup.

At first you may deny that the breakup hurts
you—or that it really happened! You may replay con-
versations over and over in your mind, stunned. You
may be really shocked that there is a big change in your
life.

In the second and third steps, you may get angry
with the ex-boyfriend or girlfriend. And at the same
time you may bargain with him or her, wanting life to
be as it used to be.

By looking at the "trauma of the dead battery" you may be better able to understand the stages of grief and loss.

If it becomes clear that the breakup is permanent, you probably will hit the fourth stage—getting depressed about it. Life may seem uncertain, and you may not know what to do.

But soon enough, you will be able to accept it, deal with it, and move on. This is the final step.

Change = Loss = Grief

Remember that loss comes to us in big and small ways. You can look at it through this equation: Change = Loss = Grief. And it can apply to both major and minor changes.

Many people in our society believe that childhood and adolescence are the happiest times of our lives. But

When you take the time to work out your grief, you may discover new things about yourself.

if Change = Loss = Grief, adolescence is the hardest time—because this is the time people go through the most change.

The most important thing to remember when you're dealing with a loss is that it's *your* process. These are simply guidelines to make it easier, and to help you understand that some emotions that come up could make you feel uncomfortable.

But these are only guidelines. That means, if you are currently going through the process of grieving and you haven't gone through the denial stage, but you are already at the anger stage, you haven't failed. It's not like taking a multiple-choice test. The right answers are the ones you discover yourself.

Writing a Contract

Whatever step you choose to take first in dealing with loss, it is the right one. It is probably also the hardest step. The first time you recognize that something in your life is causing you pain, you have, in a way, signed a silent contract with yourself that says you will move through the process.

That doesn't mean it's going to be easy or fast. But once you have admitted that you want to heal, you will have already started. It might even help to take that silent contract and put it down on paper. It can be very simple:

Dear Self,

I am writing this contract because I am committed to moving through the process of healing that I need to go through to cope with the loss of xxx. (In that space write down whatever it is that you have lost. Write it down in great detail. Don't worry if you think your loss is trivial. Write down exactly why it is important even if you think others might not agree.)

I promise to be open to my feelings, and to honor my need to cry if I should want to. I promise not to get mad at myself if I haven't finished grieving by a set time. I promise to remember that there are no rules in this process, and that whatever path I take, it is the right path.

Love,
Me

Try to look at the contract every night before you go to bed, and every morning when you wake up. Keep it in a drawer near your bed, or maybe taped up to your wall. If you're embarrassed about someone reading it, you can keep it hidden, but make sure you read it regularly.

If you feel comfortable, you could even share it with a trusted friend, parent, sibling, or therapist, and have him or her keep a copy, too. This way, if this person notices that you have abandoned your process, he or she can gently remind you that you need to get back on the path. This contract with yourself will help you remember how important it is to stay attuned to all the feelings you have about the changes in your life.

Healing a loss is like climbing a mountain. You need the proper gear and good endurance. We will explore the tools, and the paths to take on the way up, in the next chapter.

Chapter 4

The Process of Dealing with Loss

Anyone who has ever gone backpacking or rock climbing will tell you that the two most important things you should know before you head out into the wilderness are:

• Bring the proper gear.

• The most important thing is not getting to the top of the peak, but how you get there.

For our purposes, it's better to talk about the second idea first.

Sometimes, after you have lost someone or something, you want so badly to feel better again that you may move through the healing process too fast. You convince yourself that you have accomplished your goal and you are ready to move forward.

But remember, when people run up mountains, they travel too fast to notice the color of the sky, the smell

Recovering from loss may seem to take as long as climbing a mountain. But you can do it!

of the soil, or the sound of a chipmunk burrowing into a tree trunk. The view from the top of the mountain is so spectacular, they've been told, that they can't wait to get there.

However, going quickly is not always the healthiest thing. When faced with taller mountains and new journeys, people will realize that they didn't really learn anything from their experience. In fact, their trip up the mountain went so fast, and they were so out of breath when they reached the top, that they can't remember anything at all.

Mountains of Grief

It is a similar process for people who are grieving. People want to be finished with the process quickly because it can be frightening and painful, like carefully scaling a cliff.

But in dealing with loss, it is often the best thing to go slowly and look at all the different paths there are to get through your loss. This can keep you from skipping over important steps. Sometimes when you go too fast, you have no choice but to slow down.

Liz was eighteen when she got pregnant. She couldn't believe it. When she first went to the drugstore and bought the home pregnancy test with her friend Sue, she wasn't even nervous. "So, my period is two weeks late, it's no big deal," she thought. She figured she'd just take the test to be sure.

When the test came out positive, Sue was more freaked out than Liz was. She went to give her a hug but Liz just shrugged her off. Finally, Sue convinced Liz to go to the local women's health center and get an official test.

They got an appointment two days later. Liz didn't bother to tell her boyfriend, Joe. She thought he'd be really mad. She was feeling a little angry with him, too. He had convinced her that they didn't need to use a condom. He was the cutest guy in the eleventh grade and she couldn't believe that he liked her. So she mostly did what he wanted her to do. But she was beginning to feel that maybe it wasn't such a good idea.

The nurse came out of her office and called her in by name. She told her that she was seven weeks pregnant and that she had several options. Without thinking she asked how she could book an abortion. She knew a few other girls who had had the procedure done at this clinic. She wondered how she would pay. She'd have to tell Joe now, because her mom would kill her if she found out. She was thinking about all these things as the nurse gave her the appointment card. Tuesday at two-thirty.

Joe worked at the sneaker store and had some money saved up. When she told him he looked scared, and went to get the money right away. She told him not to bother coming with her, because Sue was going. He didn't understand why she sounded so unemotional.

On the day of the procedure she had a nervous pit in the middle of her belly. She thought for a second about what was inside of her, and quickly pushed the thought aside and went to meet Sue to go the clinic. When it was over she ached, but she felt relieved.

Sue asked her if she wanted to talk about it, but she told her she was really fine. The nurse at Planned Parenthood had asked her if she wanted to go to therapy but she laughed. She really thought it was no big deal.

Fast forward to five years later: Liz is in a serious relationship with a wonderful guy named Thomas. He really loves her and they are talking about having babies together after they get married. Suddenly Liz begins to sob. She tells Thomas the story of her abortion. She hasn't talked about it in five years. She wouldn't even let Sue bring it up. Thomas urges her to see a therapist. She agrees.

Before bed that night she writes down the whole story, from beginning to end. She sighs before she lies down to sleep. She didn't think it hurt that much, but now she is glad that she feels ready to face her past. It won't be easy, but it feels like the right thing.

A Step Forward, a Step Back

Liz was in denial, and not ready to make a commitment to healing her wound. For Liz, the denial stage lasted five years. The rest of the process may take a long time for her. But no matter what step she takes next, it is an important one.

The point is that now, five years later, Liz is finally committed to healing her loss. She thought that she

Some choices are very hard to make. You can help get through them by not denying your loss.

made it to the top of the mountain in no time. But when she found herself in a safe place with her boyfriend, she was forced to face the fact that she had to turn around and re-examine the path.

The Winding Path

Dealing with loss is not necessarily a one-time thing. Years after you have lost something and felt as if you were healed, you can be revisited by the pain of a loss.

You might suddenly find yourself feeling depressed or angry about losing a pet from when you were a child, even if you went through the grieving process a long time ago. Or maybe you thought you were totally over your ex-boyfriend or girlfriend. You've been dating someone new for three months. But then you run into your ex at the mall and you feel like crying again.

This is when you have to backtrack, and re-examine the path you've chosen. Perhaps you missed some trail that was better fit for you. Perhaps you weren't ready to say good-bye. Maybe you didn't achieve closure in the relationship—the official end to something.

Remembering losses is normal and healthy. You will remember losses from time to time throughout your life. Each time, you deal with them a little differently. And each time you can learn something new about yourself. The important thing is to stay in touch with your feelings.

Staying in Touch

Let's take a look back for a minute at our shortened checklist for mountain climbers.

We've already covered the second concept—paying attention to the process instead of just the end result. Now, in the next chapter, let's look at the gear we need to take with us on our journey. As you will see, there are many different ways to deal with loss. You can choose the process that feels best for you.

Chapter 5

Support Systems

After you have created your contract and you feel ready to begin your journey, one of the first steps you will have to take is selecting proper tools and finding people to help you to put those tools to use. There are countless ways for teens to help heal themselves. Let's look at a few of them.

Writing Yourself Home

One of the most helpful ways to start the process on your own is to begin keeping a journal. It helps to keep it at your bedside, or even to keep it with you all the time so that whenever you have a thought or an idea or a memory you can write it down.

It's also very helpful to write down your dreams. Everyone has dreams, even if people don't always remember them. Many people believe that we try to work out our

Writing in a journal can help you work out your feelings.

problems in our dreams. These problems sometimes come out as symbols or situations that don't even seem to make sense. But often when you write stuff down, you realize that your unconscious mind (the part of the mind you're not normally aware of) is trying to tell you something.

Sometimes people have anxiety dreams. A common one is dreaming of arriving naked to school or work. This is said to symbolize a fear of being revealed as inadequate or different. It might mean that your self-esteem is fragile. Your self-esteem is one of the most important parts of your path to healing: it's a measure of how much you value yourself.

A great way to remember your dreams is to keep a dream journal. While you are drifting off to sleep, repeat this statement to yourself over and over, "I will remember my dreams tonight, I will remember my dreams tonight . . ." Then, set your alarm for ten minutes earlier than the time you are used to waking up. This can help you remember. It is craft you can learn and get better and better at.

Talk Therapy

The most natural support system for many people is friends and family. If you can talk to someone you know and love about what is hurting you, it is always a good first step.

This is not right for everyone, however, because sometimes these are the people who are causing your pain. This is when you need to move beyond your immediate circle to some of the resources provided by your community. School, for instance, is a good place to start. Schools usually employ psychologists or social workers. If you don't know how to find the social worker or psychologist at school, ask a teacher that you trust.

Many teens choose to pursue therapy outside of school. A school social worker can refer you to an outside therapist that you can work with. If your family has health insurance, you can find a qualified therapist through your insurance company.

If you choose to pursue therapy, it helps to know what kind of therapist you are seeing. There are many different types of training.

As a result of working out your feelings, you may find it easier
to deal with your family.

- Psychologists and licensed social workers have a mas-
  ter's degree or Ph.D. in psychology and have com-
  pleted many years of additional training. They can
  conduct one-on-one therapy or lead group therapy.

- Psychiatrists are trained psychologists who also are
  medical doctors. They can do one-on-one or group
  therapy, too. But they also are authorized to prescribe
  medicine to their clients. Sometimes antidepressant
  drugs such as Prozac can be prescribed in order to
  help people who are struggling with depression.

Therapy can have many different styles. Some therapists listen closely and gently guide their patients as

they struggle with issues. Other therapists are more directive and actively give advice. You may have to look around for a little while before you find a therapy format or style that works well for you. But you'll find one!

If medication is a part of your therapy, make sure that you take it exactly as directed. Pay close attention to how the medicine is affecting you. Talk to your psychiatrist about how your feel. Remember that medication doesn't take the place of talk therapy: They work hand-in hand to help you feel better.

You can find out more about therapy through local community centers in your town, the yellow pages, the library, or even the Internet. Some Web sites that deal with grief, loss and different therapies are listed in the appendix at the end of this book.

Creative Outlets

Some therapists think that the best way to cope with pain and loss is by exploring your own creativity. Using journals or dream work is one approach. Artists trained in psychology use art therapy to help teens express themselves through painting, drawing, or sculpture.

Another kind of therapy is poetry therapy. This is something you can do on your own, or with the help of a certified poetry therapist. A lot of people get the urge to write when they feel sad. After experiencing a loss, you might feel like spilling it all out onto paper. This is part of poetry therapy, but it also involves reading poems written by other people who have experienced

The library and Internet are great places to find out more about creative ways to express yourself.

pain like yours. Sometimes it helps to read the words of others who have been there.

A fifteen-year-old girl wrote the following poem. She is an eleventh-grader at Humanities Prep High School in New York City. She wrote it in response to the sadness she felt from being separated from her family:

My Old House

The sun's warm beams
splashed on my face
as I walked fast
my Walkman full blast,

ice cracked under my feet
as I stood in front of my old house.

I looked up
almost blinded by the sun
hitting the icy snow
sending a sharp brightness
into my eyes.

I could smell
my mother's cooking,
I could hear the laughter,
and the crying.

I felt the numbers
on the house,
reading them with my hands,
the innocent curves on the 2,
and the 99
and the figure-skating 8.

I felt a rush
to bolt inside
and maybe
catch my mom and bro
laugh at me
saying it was just a joke.
But there was a new

Sometimes you may feel lonely, but if you give it time, it will pass.

family occupying
my old house,
no one to greet me.
So I turned away
from my old house
and slowly walked away,
releasing my anger
on the volume control
of my Walkman,

I turned it down
So I could hear the
ice crack as
I walked away.

Maybe I was hoping
that my old house
would say goodbye,
thanks for the memories.

But all I heard
was the ice and my own
soft sobs.
Goodbye.
Thanks for the memories.

—Chris Bautista

Chris felt better after writing this poem. It was a helpful exercise for her, and she shared it with her poetry teacher at school. She used it as a way to start exploring her feelings about loss. After she wrote the poem she was ready to openly discuss her emotions.

There are many more varieties of therapy, and the number is growing every day. If you go to self-help aisle of the bookstore you can find books on topics such as yoga therapy, wilderness therapy (think about the metaphor of "climbing the mountain"), and many others.

You have a wide range of tools available to you to cope with loss. You can use any of the resources listed here, do your own research, or contact one of the organizations listed at the end of this book.

Hope and Help

The most important thing is that you remember that you are strong enough to climb that mountain and gaze at the beautiful view. You are powerful and creative and have the rest of your life to live. Even though you face big and small losses every day, you can use them to learn just how powerful you are.

Every time you overcome loss, you are reminded that you have a lot of strength inside of you. You also have the ability to make a better world for others who might not yet know how to cope with their own losses. Remember that everything happens for a reason, and that every emotion you have is important.

Wherever you are now on your path, know that you are not alone. There are millions of people in the world

People of every generation have experienced loss and worked through it. You can, too.

who have lost and learned. Think of this group as members of your extended family. They are all working, in their own way, to overcome their losses. You can do it, too.

Glossary

addiction Dependence on a behavior or substance.

anorexia nervosa An obsessive desire to lose weight by refusing to eat.

art therapy Healing through visual arts, such as painting or drawing.

bar/bat mitzvah A rite of passage in the Jewish religion. It symbolizes the change from childhood to adulthood.

bulimia Disorder in which overeating alternates with self-induced vomiting.

closure An observed or official end to something.

coping mechanism Something that people do to make themselves feel better when they are sad or struggling.

denial Avoiding or denying the truth or existence of a situation.

ethnicity Describes a person's common cultural or national origin, such as Mexican or Italian.

physical abuse When someone is physically harmful, sometimes on a regular basis, by hitting, punching, slapping or otherwise hurting someone else in any way.

poetry therapy Healing by writing and reading poems.

psyche The soul, spirit, or mind.

psychotropic drugs Drugs such as Prozac or lithium that are prescribed by psychiatrists to treat mental illness, such as depression.

racism Prejudice grounded on a belief in the superiority of a particular race, based on ignorance.

repression The active exclusion of an unwelcome thought from conscious awareness.

rite of passage An event that marks change, growth or maturation. For instance, riding a bicycle for the first time, getting married, or starting school.

self-esteem One's sense of self-worth.

self-mutilation Disorder in which victims desire to cut, burn, or otherwise cause pain to their own bodies.

sexism Prejudice based on the belief of the superiority of men.

sexual abuse When someone sexually molests or violates someone else, often on an ongoing basis.

socialization A term used by sociologists to describe the way individuals adhere to the norms of their culture or the way they behave in groups.

unconscious The normally inaccessible part of the mind affecting the emotions.

verbal abuse When someone verbally assaults another person, by yelling or simply by saying things that undermine the abused individual's self-esteem.

For Further Reading

Bode, Janet. *Death Is Hard to Live With: Teenagers Talk About How They Cope with Loss.* New York: Delacorte Press, 1994.

Canfield, Jack. *Chicken Soup for the Teenage Soul: 101 Stories of Life, Love and Learning (Chicken Soup for the Soul Series).* New York: Health Communications, 1997.

Glass, George. *Drugs and Fitting In.* New York: The Rosen Publishing Group, 1998.

Kubersky. Rachel. *Everything You Need to Know About Eating Disorders*, Rev. ed. New York: The Rosen Publishing Group, 1996.

Kubler-Ross, Elisabeth. *The Wheel of Life: A Memoir of Living and Dying.* New York: Scribner, 1997.

McKoy, Kathy, and Charles Wibbelsman, M.D. *Life Happens: A Teenager's Guide to Friends, Failure,*

Sexuality, Love . . . . NewYork: Berkley Publishing, 1996.

Ng, Gina. *Everything You Need to Kow About Self-Mutilaion: A Helping Guide for Teens Who Hurt Themselves.* New York: The Rosen Publishing Group, 1998.

Where To Go For Help

TAG: Teen Age Grief, Inc.
P.O. Box 220034
New Hall, CA 91322-0034
(805) 253-1932
email: tag@smartlink.net
web site: http://www.smartlink.net/~tag/

Therapy FAQ-(Frequently Asked Questions)
e-mail: mmiles@abulafia.st.hmc.edu
Web site: http://abulafia.st.hmc.edu/~mmiles/
    noframes.html

Webster's Death, Dying & Grief Home Page
e-mail: webster@katsden.com
Web Site: http://www.katsden.com/death/index.html

People With AIDS Coalition-PWAC
50 West 17th Street
8th floor
New York, NY 10011
(212) 647-1415
e-mail: hivinfo@nyam.org
Web Site: http://www.aidsnyc.org/pwac/letters.html

Virtual Pet Cemetery (Web Site for people grieving for their pets)
Web Site: http://www.lavamind.com/pet.html

Covenant House
A safe haven for kids who are hurting. You can call to talk from anywhere in the world.
(800) 999-9999
Email: http://www.covenanthouse.org/kid/kid.htm

Index

About The Author

Stefanie Iris Weiss is a teacher and writer living in Greenwich Village with her bewitching 6-year-old cat, Caboodle. Her passions are poetry and teaching writing to young people. She is currently writing a book about spirituality for women in their twenties.

Photo Credits

Photo on p. 2 by Lauren Piperno; pp. 8, 20, 27, 42, 44 by Ira Fox; p. 10 by Douglas Peebles; pp. 12, 15, 24, 31, 32, 39, 50 by Ryan Giuliani; p. 22 by Barbara Peacock; p. 36 by Lowell Georgia; p. 48 by Ethan Zinder; p. 53 by Steve Raymer.